Anxious Thoughts

from an

Awkward Mind

katarina illona

To Erik: my daily reminder to work hard and push past my limits to
be the best version of myself I can be. I love you...
ten billion percent!

To my parents: my constant role models who show the importance of
helping others and giving back to the community, to put more good in
the world. I treasure that you are my parents, and I love you both.

To my family: my happiness that inspires a twinkle in my heart...
I wouldn't trade our memories for anything. Even unlimited pizza!

To my friends: my supporters and test-readers that constantly share
memes and words of encouragement with me, so I know my work
doesn't entirely stink. ;)

I love, admire and appreciate all of you more than you know.

Also...

To those who have taught me valuable life lessons at a painful price -
I'll acknowledge that even *you* have played a part in my growth.

Table of Contents

Introduction
Poetry is Me

Just like the human mind, which can sometimes resemble a computer browser with 17 open tabs and random music playing, this collection of poems includes everything. And I mean everything!

Following my own chaotic mind, hurried along by anxiety that sometimes keeps me up at night, this shaped the bones of my first poetry collection. Although, I shouldn't complain. Those quiet, late nights lying in bed bathed in moonlight are often when I create the poems I'm most fond of.

If you are looking for one theme of poetry to explore, then this collection might not be quite what you're looking for. But that's okay! There are no rules for reading this collection of thoughts and reflections. Browse in whatever order you'd like. Or let the moment inspire you! These poems do not build off each other nor do they need to be read in a specific order.

If you're feeling a little down and want encouragement for expressing some self-love, I recommend skipping ahead to section two. This focuses on acknowledging our strengths and great qualities. Maybe it will inspire you to think about what positive things you contribute to the world! And that everyone deserves to speak kindly to themselves. (Unless you're a jerk. Then maybe rethink how you treat others.)

However, if you're having a rough day and would like to wallow in self-pity (we've all been there, it's allowed) maybe get started with section one. I've found sometimes it helps to read reaffirming words to know you're not alone in how you're feeling. Like blaring sad music on repeat for a while.

Or, if you're not interested in any particular emotions to evoke, feel free to skip to section three: people, places and things! This explores everything and anything. Sometimes scenes in nature or life resonate in my soul and I *have* to capture it in a poem. Sometimes, people leave an impact on me…good or bad. And sometimes, I ponder the future. I told you: everything and anything lies within!

And last, but not least, are micro poems. I'm less than five feet tall. So these poems, like me, are small but mighty! These brief thoughts are meant to be easily digestible.

I truly hope you enjoy this collection.

My goal is that you read this and feel all good things: a sense of validation, acknowledgement, encouragement, support…all great things that we yearn for in life.

-katarina illona

Introduction

Hello,
It's nice to meet you.
I should introduce myself
however,
it's likely that
I would panic,
and stumble over
words like
"Hi, I'm anxious".
I'd say that,
Rather that enlighten you
on the name that my parents
so very meticulously selected
as the beginning of my
carefully curated identity -
Rather than introduce myself,
as someone worthy of
noteworthy traits,
I'd most likely
reduce myself to
a single flaw.

*

Poetry is Me

poetry is not just
writing

it is an
expression
of myself,
putting my soul
onto paper

it is the
pouring
of my emotions
like an overflowing jug
of water
nourishing the earth

it is a
microscope
by which to
explore the smallest atoms
of my being

it is a
breath
of air that
breathes life into
my name
my self
my story

poetry is
me

*

Section 1: Reflection

Sometimes I don't always like myself. And that's okay.

There are some days when I feel like I am on top of the world. I can do anything I want, anything I touch turns to gold and I enchant everyone that I come across with my delightful quirkiness. But then there are days where I take, "we are our own worst critic" to a whole new level. When I am so unpleasant to myself and borderline bully my own mind.

To make matters worse, on these days where I think the absolute worst of myself, I will then harass myself with thoughts like, "why are you even acting like this?" and "why can't you just be kind to yourself?". The worst is when I manipulate myself. "If YOU can't be nice to yourself, why should others?" Great point, me.

What I've realized is that in order to embrace myself, I first need to understand who I am, what I stand for, and what lies within my heart and mind. Once I understand and acknowledge this, I can move forward accordingly.

Simplified: I cannot love myself until I know myself. And, unfortunately, sometimes that means acknowledging myself. All of it. The good, the bad, and the ugly.

And here it is, in poem form.

*

Band-Aids

I wish they made
bandaids
for mental health,
a temporary fix
I could slap on
to help
keep myself going.

But mental health cures
don't always come
in the form of
princess patterns and
cartoon characters.

Bricks

There are some lies
I've told myself
Over the years -
   I was unworthy
     my soul was broken
      that I meant nothing to this world
I didn't notice that
I used these lies like bricks
creating a wall around me
until it was too late.
I was blocked in,
shielded away
from those who might hurt me
if I chose to let them in.

But I'm specific with the pain I allow -
I would rather my loneliness
strike my heart like an arrow
than someone's actions
pierce my back like a blade.

Borrowing

What a way
to live life
constantly borrowing from
    tomorrow
in order to make it through
    today.
To crawl across the finish line
inch by inch
barely making it through
the challenges of the day,
only to be expected
to meet tomorrow
fully re-charged
and ready to
outdo myself,
each and every day.

Character

How dynamic and vast are my skills
as an actress,
not only to have the ability
to play the hero in my story:
brave, courageous and
full of compassion -
but also the villain in
another's story:
cunning, cruel, heartless
and whatever other
adjectives have been
associated with my character.

Yet,
I make peace with the fact that
while yes,
I choose the part I would like to play
in my own narrative -
others decide how they cast
the ensemble in their story.
I am merely assigned a part,
whether I've auditioned or not.

Chasin'

It feels like
anxiety is chasin' me
like a romance author
and a good love story.
A tale as old as time,
unyielding,
unwavering,
and reliable.
Some things just never change.

Cookie Cutter

Grow up.
Land a job.
Get married.
Start a family.
Wash, Rinse, Repeat
it seems to be
for each and every person.
But should that really
be the case?
Yeah,
life can be like
a box of chocolates,
and all that.
But,
it's also a puzzle
and each person holds their
own unique solution.
I love cookies, but
a cookie cutter life
doesn't sound like
it's for me.

Cracked

Like a cracked windshield I am
broken
delicate
and nearly shattered
trying desperately to
hold it all together

Yet somehow
I am still able
to reflect the light
that shines on me.

Cycle

There is a
vicious cycle
in
mental Health

I come to realize
my mind is working
against me
performing a cha-cha with
one step forward, then
ten steps back.

I ask for help.
sometimes my assistance
comes
in the form of
regulated
professional
    conversation.
Sometimes my assistance
comes
in the form of
a pill to
grace the top of my tongue

I grow.
I change.
I thrive.
as the desired effects take
place.

My confidence soars like
Icarus,
on wings of medicated
serotonin.
I climb
    higher
    and
        higher
away from the medication,
until I
come crashing down
to rock bottom
and realize I need the help
again.

Wash. Rinse. Repeat.
never to break the cycle.

Dark Place

I feel like I have been
stumbling through my life
without a purpose,
trapped within darkness
with no chance of
freeing myself from this
prison-like state.
Only with the discovery
of a passion,
a drive by which
I make a difference and
contribute to the world,
can I find a light
to lead my life -
guiding me from this
dim and lifeless place.

Dictionary

More than 400,000 entries
in Webster's dictionary,
    and yet
there are still moments
that words
    fail to describe.
When no carefully woven sentence,
    nor eloquent expression
can accurately capture
what my heart
is trying to convey.

Drowning

Weighed down by
my past discretions -

How am I supposed to
embrace my new and improved self,
when I am shackled by
my past mistakes,
like a skin I cannot shed.

How am I supposed to grow,
emerging from my cocoon
a new and better person
if I cannot free myself
from the weight of my past sins?

Fixing You

When will I remember,
that no matter
how much I yearn to,
I cannot give part of myself
to complete you
if it means leaving myself bare,
missing parts -
unable to function.
I cannot share a
puzzle piece with another
if it means I am a missing set.

A porcelain doll, with
delicate skin trapping
a demon, lurking inside.
"You are so cute!"
and
"What a sweetheart"
they say,
like a self-fulfilling prophecy
could actually happen for me.
I play the part,
the world my stage as I
portray the good little girl
that everyone assumes me
to be.
When I feel drenched in sadness,
I'm met with surprise as,
"But you seem so happy!"
floods my senses.
My fragile outer layer
is made of paper mache,
hiding an unexpected darkness
that lies within.

Language

It's like I
need a translator
to accurately express
the swirling storm of
thoughts and emotions,
like resounding
   GONGS
within my head
echoing with every second
they cannot escape my mind -
like thieves from a crime scene.
Trapped within my mind,
it feels like no words
in my mother tongue
can free these feelings from my
mental Terror Dome.
But I don't need Rosetta Stone
to know that no words
ever will.

Moving Mountains

Just because I carry myself
with the strength to move mountains
and
carry the world upon my back,
does not mean that I should.

Nor that I deserve to.

They say that
God gives his toughest battles,
to the toughest soldiers.

But what if I
did not sign up to serve?

Repeat

My brain feels broken,
stuck on repeat
with obsessive thoughts.
Unwelcome and unnecessary thoughts, like
guests that invited themselves into a home,
and refuse to leave.

I think about the laundry left unfolded.
I think about the dishes left untouched in the sink.
I think about the books piled on the bookshelf, waiting to be
read.
I think intrusive thoughts that I cannot stop, nor can I control.

I cannot pilot my own mind,
I am merely a passenger,
trying to survive the turbulence
of my mental illness.

Shades of Red

While I admit,
red is a lovely color for
complimenting my complexion,
the reality
is that red is
a *terrible* color on me.

My heart, bathed in
a deep red coat of
shimmering frustration
and anger,
bubbles in intensity
until the intense shade
takes over my vision,
drenching everything in a
disgusting and volatile shade
of anger.

I try to avoid red,
where and when I can.
But sometimes
I run out of other colors
To clothe my heart.

Treading Water

I am treading water
In a sea of anxiety.
Waves crash around me
    And yet
I somehow manage to find the strength
To float and
    Weather the storms in my mind

Shattered

Here I stand
holding my shattered heart
held within my skin -
like a bandaid.
Hoping its enough
to heal
what cannot be undone.

Strength

You'd think that
I would be much stronger,
   for how much I
carry you
in my heart,
each and every day.
And yet,
my walls still crumble
    when I see you
       smile.

Why Do I

Why do I -
Show unconditional love to others
showering them with
love, affection, encouragement,
without leaving a drop for myself.
Without enveloping myself in the
rejuvenating thoughts, and healing ideas.

Why do I -
Praise others as if
The words I speak are
water on the tongue of a parched mouth.
Yet, I leave myself lost in a desert,
dry and brittle as a wilted flower,
ready to snap with a breath of the wind.

Why do I -
Forgive the actions and wrongdoings of others,
comparing them to sweet children who
do not know of their mistakes.
While I condemn myself
to a lesser life, for merely being human-
Perfectly imperfect.

"Once I get life together and my confidence grows, it's over for all of you!" -Me, probably.

There are countless quotes, wallpapers, posters and viral social media statuses encouraging us to be kind to one another - so why not include ourselves? When kind words or thoughtful actions are so often praised when offered to other people, why do we cringe when we speak it for ourselves?

I think it's because, unfortunately, not enough people are kind enough to themselves. That when we do see it, people assume it's an overinflated ego. Not genuine pride for someone who has grown to be an even better version of who they were.

So, it's time to break that. Reflect on ourselves and acknowledge the amazing things we do for others, the personality we bring to the world and the memories we help create. Empower yourself to say, "wait a second - I'm actually a really fun person!" Or whatever positive adjective you'd like to choose.

But the key is to not gaslight yourself into thinking you're being vain. There is a huge difference between someone bragging about something, versus someone taking pride in who they are or what they bring to the world!

My challenge to you, is to think about what you'd brag to others about...featuring yourself! Positive answers only!

Think of the following poems as my responses to that challenge.

*

Access Denied

You have no right
to know the person I am now
   Since you left.
the growth I have experienced
the confidence I have carefully nurtured
   like a delicate seed
the love with which I have nourished others hearts, even my
own
I thrive.
I am…
   a book, with words that will not dance through your
thoughts
   a scene your eyes do not have permission to view
   a melody to never grace your ears.
I am new.

Affection

I am a cat.
Bask in the glory of
my wonder,
and show me love.
I prefer affection
on my own terms.
Meet me where I am,
speaking a language
with your actions
that my ears prefer to hear.

Always Here

I am always here.
When it is convenient for you.
When it suits you.
When it makes you look better.
When I have a part to play.
When it satisfies a role.
I'm always here.
But,
what you might not know
is that I am here, even
when you are elsewhere,
when the space around me is blank.
whether you realize my worth, or not.
I'm always here.

breathing

smiling

existing

making a difference in this world,
weaving melodies of memories with souls that
make up the symphony of my life.
Creating a canvas of relationships,
splattered with the colors of my favorite souls.
Even when you aren't,
I am always here.

<u>I Crawl Along</u>
Here I am,
crawling along the ground
at the feet of others.
I know I should fly
but I am not there yet.
There is still far to go
on my journey of
who I am meant to be.

<u>Enclose Me in Possibilities</u>
I surround myself in
the cocoon of knowledge
and lessons I have learned
the hard way
ready to become my final form.
Enclose me in possibilities
and watch me grow.

<u>Spread My Wings</u>
I am a butterfly
and have shed my
shell of insecurities.
I have transformed into
my true self.
Now,
it's time to spread my wings
and fly on these
new wings of
authenticity and beauty.

Cha Cha

We are trained to believe
that only moving forward
should be celebrated as "progress".

But, is not
stopping for rest
and careful reflection
also
crucial for growth?

I can be
proud of myself,
celebrating my achievements
and admiring proud moments
while also
holding myself accountable
for my stumblings and
self-reprimanding any
misgivings,
trying to use all of these feelings
to transform into
the best version of myself
that I can be.

Sometimes,
a cha-cha can be fun -
the graceful combination
of forward and backward movement
in an ongoing and
magnificent process
of growth worth celebrating.

Cracked and Beautiful

Like a deep crack
running along beautiful
and intricately etched glass,
or frozen ice waiting to
crack through the middle
from the pressure -
there can be a delicate beauty
in the face of
danger and catastrophe.
Look at how
flames dance
as they destroy.

Cry & Kickass

Just like
    sweet and salty
    sugar and spice
there is a power in duality,
to toe the line, knowing when to
show kindness and mercy
    with the patience of a saint
or
demonstrate the strength of a force to
    be reckoned with.
I can cry and still be kickass,
just give me the right time and place to
    show you both.

Delicate

I am delicate.
But do not misunderstand,
it is a particular kind
of delicate.

It is not the fragile state of
a budding flower,
ready to split apart from
the simplest touch.

Instead, it is the fragile state of
a resting bomb,
waiting to ignite from
the perfect provocation.

It is not weakness, but an
unrelenting strength.
So hear me, when I say that
I am a particular kind of delicate.

Doodle

How kind of you
to have taken the time
to create a version of me,
one that exists only
in your mind.
Even though
I've worked meticulously
through the years
to create this masterpiece of
a self, through
surviving the heartbreaks,
maneuvering the frustrations
and
overcoming the obstacles
put in my path,
you've created your own
rough draft, summarizing a snippet of
brief, woefully incorrect, perceived interactions.
But masterpieces can never
truly be authentically recreated,
leaving a lesser quality copy
ever darkening the shadows…
In this case,
the shadow of your mind.
A doodle will never
outshine the Mona Lisa.

Forging my Throne

I have spent
many years
   carefully
   and
   meticulously
forging my throne
upon which I sit -
heated through anger
and plunged into water,
desperately grasping for
any sense of semblance
or normalcy.
Gradually tempered
and shaped through
   grueling work,
    the agony of betrayal,
     the pain that life brings.
This intense process -
only to be repeated
time and time again,
with the labors that
the world has to offer.
Until,
emerging from the forge,
   stronger,
   sharper,
   defined,
I sit on the throne of
my past trauma,
to rule over my life
and future
to come.

Growing

Who says that
growing in
feet
and
inches
is the only significant
or worthy
way to grow?
That strengthening my
capacity for love
or increasing the height
of my potential
is not just as
incredible?
That bettering my capacity for
empathy and affection,
or decreasing my
disposition for
overthinking until
my mind is raw,
is not worthy of
joyous celebration?
I may be
stuck
in an unchangeable
4'10.5"
until my body withers and shrinks with age,
but
the best of my growth
is still yet to come.

Ingredients

I don't like ricotta cheese,
but I really do love lasagna.
While vegetables aren't my favorite,
    chicken pot pie
fills not only my stomach,
but my heart as well -
    like warming bones on a winter's day.

We all have a part to play,
    each a key ingredient to life.
So while you may not like
the flavor I bring,
you cannot deny
my contribution to this dish of life.

I Am

I am...
a lot of things.
A cornucopia of
unique experiences,
quirky characteristics,
undeniable enthusiasm
and a love of laughter.
all combined together to
create a soul as unique as the
stars and moon I so lovingly gaze upon.
I am...
caring.
passionate.
optimistic.
a lot of things.
And
I am me.
and that's enough.

I Close My Door

What if
the lock keeping the door to life
from opening
to wonderful possibilities,
has been me
all along?
Using my fear of
rejection
    and
failure,
molding it into an unbreakable lock
that nothing could hope to demolish...
keeping me in a false sense
of safety.

Was this a coping mechanism?
Or was this
just a way,
I didn't know that
I was holding myself back?

Well,
I think it's time
for me to outgrow the room
I've isolated myself in.
To grow my confidence
and lessen my fear.
Now,
the chance of opportunity,
and clean slate
will be the
shiniest gold key
to open the lock.

I Will Rise

The best part about me
is that
I cannot
and
will not
go away,
fading into nothingness.
I may fall,
stumbling in the darkness
as I try to find my way,
but I will always
get back up.
Like a phoenix
scorched in the magnificent flames,
and burned into ashes,
I emerge.
I rise.
I start over
attempting anew.
I will always get back up.

Pressure

No matter how much pressure
you put on me
or the stress
I'm subjected to
I will survive
stronger
and more
beautiful
than ever.
Pressure creates
diamonds and darling,
I'm more carats
than you deserve.

Progress

I may not be
in my final form,
but I am still a masterpiece
in the making.
Although it's not
yet complete
and there is still work
to be done,
my efforts are
just as magnificent
as the results.

Rebuilt

When you broke me down
I shattered into countless pieces that had to be carefully
    put back into place,
like delicate fabric coming together

Slowly, I stitched each piece in place
with exhibitions of self love,
cultivated carefully and meticulously.

Then you were replaced
with someone who was ready to treasure a
    perfectly imperfect
    and flawed woman.

You saw a
    broken
    misshapen
    mess
that could be shattered with the simplest thought

He saw a
    beautiful
    unique
    lovingly created collection of
    memories, held together by a passion for love and
the desire to express it.

Stained Glass

Although I have been broken
time and time again,
my heart and soul
shattered into
a chaotic mess of
countless pieces
I will
put them together again
to create a stained glass masterpiece
of my life
so that my trials may
fracture light
into a magnificent array colors

Tacos Fall Apart

Tacos are
still loved,
despite
   shells breaking.
despite
   falling apart.
despite
   being a complete mess.
So why
my friend,
shouldn't we still be loved?

Temple

I have been
beautifully
and
meticulously
created,
shaped carefully and wondrously
like a potter and clay
bringing to life another creation.

I am a beautiful temple
with pristine floors,
marble walls,
and alabaster sculptures
representing my memories.

Yet,
the walls echo with brutal
thoughts against myself,
that desecrate the space with
toxic words,
slicing my sculptures in two
and coating the walls
with self-deprecating filth.

The state of my temple
is more than a face-mask
or bubble bath can cleanse.

Toxic Words

It's time for me to change the tune
to morph the words
I direct at myself.
To change the sour-coated words
that sting like barbed wire,
into healing words, coated in honey
that lift me higher
than any platform wedges ever could.

Section 3: People, Places and Things

Be here. Be still. Be part of the world.

Sitting outside a coffee shop, as I add to this collection, I'm struck by a sense of...being. In a busy world where everyone is hurrying off to the next thing, not taking the time to look both ways, share a moment for a kind word or even stop and look at the sky, I am reminded it isn't always easy.

But sometimes, in the right environment, it is easy.

As I feel the gentle breeze dance across my face, leaves swirling next to me, I'm reminded that we are all part of this wide and wild world. We all have a part to play. Unfortunately, some roles are less pleasant than others. But, just as it takes all types of callings to make the world go 'round, so too, is it in this case.

So, when I can, I like to sit and be. Soak up the sunlight like a cat, listen to the sounds beside me and absorb the wonder of the world all around. To recharge my battery - so I'm ready to go out and make a difference in the world.

There are enough bad things that happen. Every day. But, the least we can do is try and put good into the world. One smile, or kind word, at a time.

*

Actions

Show your love
in a way
that if
actions speak louder
than words,
your efforts
shout affection
from the rooftops.

Be Better

Strive to be someone
your younger self would
    admire
with a zeal to set the world ablaze.

Strive to be someone
that inspires
    change
in a world full of hurt and sorrow,
begging for love.

Strive to be someone
    always wanting to be better.

Closing Tabs

Sometimes,
when life feels too overwhelming,
burdened down by
the stress and anxiety
of daily tasks
it's time to

Ctrl+Alt+Delete.

To force shut down
the many tabs that
your mind has running
at full speed in different directions -
clogging up your energy and
confounding your senses.
To finally pause the music that,
if we're being honest,
you probably don't know
where it's coming from anyway.
Starting over with
a clean slate,
and empty mind
when there was once confusion or conflict,
isn't giving up.
It's growing up.

Contributors Wanted

I am accepting contributors
to add to my story.
Authors -
    spinning webs
made of carefully crafted words of support,
and meticulous feelings of love.
Artists -
    mixing golden hues of happiness
    and
twinkling, shimmery shades of laugher
creating a canvas of memories.
Storytellers -
    passing along the wisdom and lessons
learned the hard way from my pain
    and
heartbreak, over the years.

For although I may fade,
the anthology of my legacy
    will live on.

Dandelions

I will sprout kindness everywhere,
surrounding me
like dandelions
dancing on the breeze.
Let people make beautiful wishes
so these blooms may spread.

Darkness

The night is the hardest.
I lie awake
with nothing but my obsessive internal dialogue
acting as a lullaby to soothe me to sleep.
There is nothing relaxing about the racing thoughts
that come
    one by one,
    line by line,
    piece by piece,
Slowly edging away any sliver of slumber that threatens my
mind,
that could potentially relieve me
of this emotional terror,
while I scour
    every cringey social interaction,
    every missed opportunity for a clever retort,
    every time I did not advocate for myself,
    every time my body and mind
        were not allowed to rest...
or
    every self-loathing thought, laced with poison
        eroding myself from the inside out
        despite knowing that *I deserve better.*
I am tired.
Rather than an empty sky, twinkling with stars
of possibilities, my mind prefers to see
a dark abyss full of every "worst case scenario"
my brain can possibly create -
constantly outdoing itself
(a feat not worth celebrating.)

Etch-a-Sketch

With a gentle shake,
I could start anew -
A clean slate
helps to appreciate
the opportunity for a do-over.
If only life
could be so fulfilling
in giving
me the chance to
fix my mistakes

shake

shake

shake

for a blank canvas
to try again.
Alas,
this isn't how it work
and I'm forced to
live with what I've done,
with no chance to start over.

Happily Ever After

Not ever happily ever after
looks like
a horse riding off into the sunset -
a final destination of
paradise and eternal happiness.
Sometimes,
instead
the journey to get there
is all the happily ever after you'll need.

Heart's Melody

My memories of you
are like a melody
my heart sings when I daydream -
a symphony of
allegro arpeggios and
tremendous trills
all coming together to create
a masterpiece befitting
to our love.

Ingredient

You are not a recipe missing
a single ingredient
to complete it.

You are a dish
cooked to perfection,
awaiting only the smallest topping
to enhance
your flavor

You are enough
without them.
They should only complement
what you
already are.

Kindness

I will
create a canvas of kindness
within the world.

Holding the paintbrush
with the strength and endurance
that I use, clinging to
my most cherished memories,

Using my carefully cultivated
memories to add the
gradient of magnificent colors

I will
create a canvas of kindness
within the world and
love will be my muse.

Lemonade

I am tired of making lemonade,
overburdened with the task of
making the most out of what life throws at me.
What was once refreshing optimism,
has now spoiled into sickeningly sweet foolishness.

I am drowning in the lemonade
that I so carefully and meticulously created
with all the lemons
gifted to me.

Like the Moon

We change
We morph
We transform
with our beauty we inspire
like the moon
We mesmerize
We enchant others
even in our darkness.

I hope that
God notices the little things,
like the way my speechless gaze
cannot tear itself away from your
bewitching smile, entranced by the way
the sound of your voice tickles my heart.

I hope that
God notices the little things,
watching while my chest heaves as I
catch my breath, laughter
overcoming me,
overpowering any sense of dread
or anxiety, and instead letting
a wave of peace wash over my soul.

I hope that
God notices the little things,
seeing the twinkle in my eye that
dazzles brighter than diamonds in the sun
when I am around you,
inspiring a smile more genuine
than anything I've experienced before.

I hope that
God notices the little things,
because they utter a more
eloquent prayer of appreciation for you,
than my mere words ever could.

New Chapters

I love the smell of a new book.

But it isn't the smell of
   fresh paper,
   or
   the leather bound cover,
   waiting to be opened and explored.
Instead,
it is the
   limitless possibilities
that await between the pages
bursting at the seams of a
book's spine, ready to be experienced.
Could it be
the decadent aroma of
a joyous feast,
celebrating a hero's triumphant return from war?
Could it be
the heavy fumes of molten metal,
sliced by plasma blades,
in an effort to topple
a delicate empire.
Or,
Could it be…
the intoxicating scent of perfume,
donned in hopes of
tantalizing and enchanting.
One will never know,
what scent a book may hold
until the pages are opened
and adventure is seized.

Night Owl

There is a magic
alive in the world
when
    everything sleeps
    except for me

I bask in the moonlight that
dances around,
bringing the space around me alive
with
    curiosity and
    the limitless opportunities that await.

The world, brought to a standstill
seems cloaked
in an illusion of peace and respite,
if only
    for a short while.

So yes, it's true
That I shudder at the dark.
But
    I do not fear the night.

Rebirth

What if you had the opportunity
to start over?
To be reborn
with the world at your fingertips?
A blank canvas,
with every color and shade represented
in the form of all the
pencils,
charcoals,
pastel,
paints of every variety
waiting
to create art and life
from nothing.
How will you blend the pencils,
for the perfect gradient,
bringing together people from all walks of life?
How do you plan to
Drag the paintbrushes across canvas,
creating beauty and friendship
out of nothing more than
the souls around you?
Will you plan your
hopes,
dreams,
goals
via a careful initial sketch
smudging charcoal as you create?
There are many mediums
with which to create,
it's up to you
to decide how you use
the materials given to you.

Speaking Love

Let us be kind to ourselves
by changing the narrative,
speaking love like a mantra.

I am not broken,
  I am growing and learning from my past.

I am not weak,
  I am moving mountains with my kindness.

I am not flawed,
  I am living my most perfectly imperfect life,
with a soul unique enough to call
    my own.

Trapped

Sometimes
it is not a matter of
whether or not
the light is out there
waiting to illuminate and
brighten our chosen path
but rather -
whether or not
we are willing to reach out
and take hold.
We trap ourselves in darkness,
and then ache for the light -
not realizing that we are
our worst critic,
and obstacle,
we yearn to overcome.

Tree

I am a tree.
I give shelter, support
    and life
to those around me,
surrounding them with
my peaceful embrace.
I grow and change
with the seasons
emitting my beautiful colors
as life goes on.
Sometimes, my leaves
let go, and twirl away
upon the wind
as loved ones become distant memories -
etched into my heart
by the claws that
so painfully yanked them away.
But,
I survive.
I mourn the loss with my bare branches,
moving forward with broad shoulders
and an unmovable foundation
that keeps me from shattering
to my core.

What Awaits?

When I close my eyes
I'm met not with
darkness
but with an emptiness
that suggests new possibilities,
an open space that allows for
limitless opportunities
ready for me
to choose a path.
Who knows
what adventures await on the horizon
what vast lands itch to be explored
what memories long to be created.
It is up to me to find out,
all beginning
with open eyes
and
a step forward.

Wishes

If you ever wonder
how much I love you,
Just remember remember
how much care
goes into making the perfect wish
on a shooting star.

Section 4: Micropoems

Why is a
happily ever after
only something
people find in stories?
Or, are we each just
a different narrative
being lived out loud?

*

I will not translate my narrative
into words
you are willing to hear

*

When do I throw in the towel
and decide to cease
cleaning my glasses -
since I've seen enough.

Why are the bloom of good deeds
often overpowered
by sour repercussions,
coating my tongue
with perfect hindsight?

*

My eyes flutter shut
as I drift off to sleep,
enveloped in the false security
and the reassurance
your lies offer.

*

I owe an apology
to those I've lied to
over the years,
while I paraded behind
a false identity.
But the biggest apology goes to myself,
for not being my
authentic self sooner.

Falling for you
like leaves from a tree -
let us dance on the breeze
as we journey together.

*

Tears slide down my face,
as I watch you claw your way ahead,
with nails that have been sharpened
by the backs of others
you've met along the way.
Even my back holds scars.

*

Isn't it incredible how
my words can shatter others
yet my tone can also soothe?
It is the purpose with which we use
our gift of speech,
that we either bless or break.